Library of
Davidson College

LOOSE ENDS

John Hewitt

The Blackstaff Press

821
H611l

British Library Cataloguing in Publication Data

Hewitt, John *19—*
　Loose ends.
　I. Title
　821'.914　　　PR6058.E/

　ISBN　0-85640-284-2

© John Hewitt 1983

Published by The Blackstaff Press Limited
3 Galway Park, Dundonald, BT16 0AN,
with the assistance of
The Arts Council of Northern Ireland

All rights reserved

86-4120

Printed in Northern Ireland
by Belfast Litho Printers Limited

For Jean

Dear girl, dream daughter of the childless years —
known all your days — of such a surrogate,
of her too, hearthstone of my prime's estate,
staff, anchor, buttress, when beset by cares —
those forty vivid years none living shares —
till riven from me by a witless fate
when I most needed, older grown; so great
a sheaf of masks your single visage wears.

When, that bright day, chance brought beneath my roof
you and your sons, I snatched at the relief,
a sounding house to stem my lonely grief.
Now, six years later, with the daily proof
of this assuagement, to your bracing care,
may these brief lines my lucky debt declare.

August 1982

Contents

North West Passage: an old man dying	1
The reference	2
The portrait	4
A difficult man	7
Drypoint	8
The test	10
Calling on Peadar O'Donnell at Dungloe	12
The ballad	13
The clink of rhyme	15
Folk custom	16
MacDonnell's question	17
The house on the hill	18
This Antrim air in summer	21
Autumn gale	22
The old mill-race	23
The descent	24
The souterrain	25
Palimpsest	26
The Christmas Rhymers, Ballynure 1941	27
Encounter with R.J. Welch, the antiquary	28
The house at Ballyholme	29
My widowed mother	30
Bandstand	31
For Roberta in the garden	32
The hedgehog: for R.	33
At the newsagent's	34
The bombed public house	36
Executives third tier	37
Administration	38
By air to Birmingham on a mid June evening	39
Rotterdam	42
To the People of Dresden	43
Winter park	44
On the preservation of work sheets	45
Dissertation I	46
Dissertation II	47

In recollection of Drumcliffe, September 1948	48
First honey	49
Retreaded rhymes	50
Lines for a dead alderman	51
St Stephen's Day	52
Notes	53

North West Passage: an old man dying

Tired now both mind and body, bearings loose,
he meshes into meaning now and then
when an old cog engages. If you press
it turns with logic. Let his attention wander,
it slips out of the true and spins away,
inventing sentences like 'It's a pity
the boy hadn't reached that stage before he was
challenged by the poetry. . .' I too
am challenged by the stubborn will of words
that, linked by their own law, communicate
an argument that seems an armature
for some new structure for the searching mind.
Which linked these words? Was he the unnamed boy?
And at what stage? And whose the poetry?
Is this some flicker of talk yesterday
when the page prompted and the verse leapt out
of its dead classroom context long forgotten?
Yet this spins free from any text we shared.

Ignoring his long illness and his weakness,
he's just returned who never left his bed,
proposes rising, calls to one not there,
or plucks the quilt blind-fingered, though grasps firm
for greeting or goodbye, accepting either:
shadow is substance, substance shadow, time
irrelevant, sound actual on what level.

The hulk's swamped. As the wheel whirls out of hand,
awash the vessel drifts in mountainous seas,
with tattered signals we've no skill to read.

The reference

We hadn't met for six or seven years,
a slight lad then, his eyes, his mind shone bright
with dreams of social justice, of revolution;
his being stripped for action, his thought single,
clean as a bow strung tense for its intention;
with none of the crippling harness of the world
to halt or hobble him. Neither girls nor cars,
career or hobby, love of success or money,
trap of domestic comfort, to divert
his frank gaze from the first faint hint of dawn.

And I had envied him his youth, his dream,
my own dream not dissimilar but blurred
with too much reading, of liking, of indulgence
in what I always think my loyalties,
his sheer lack of self-interest, his open heart.

I'd known he'd crammed the six years' interval
with pickets, strike committees, protest meetings,
strident west and south at factory gates,
bannered now and then with demonstrations.
I'd seen his name thread through the flimsy sheets
I read at times to prick my sagging hopes,
signed to some blunt and turgid article
in the numb jargon of his rigid sect.
I'd thought the mould was set. He'd edge away
along the margin of my politics,
fixed, doctrinaire, among the gales of time
that whisk the wilting answers from our lips.

Then he arrived to ask my signature
as casually as one might beg a match
from someone passing, neighbour in a queue.
A man now, six years older, he had not lost
the brightness of the eyes, the friendly smile,
not puffed or stuffed with ready rhetoric,

glib-lipped with party clichés in his talk,
gentler perhaps, maybe a thought less urgent.
My envy now was spiced with admiration,
still undefeated, not grown cynical,
the dream survived intact, the trapping rocks
his course was mixed with had been navigated.

He knew the men he'd worked with, virtues, faults.
He hoped to stand aside now for a year
to weigh and finger his experience,
take stock, decide how best he could be used
and what he'd need to learn to meet that use.

So, for this once, he'd need a reference
to buy the time in this unvexing job
he'd fixed his mind on. So I signed the form.
Were he my son I should be satisfied.

The portrait

Up the damp gravelled drive as the laurels dripped,
grating on pebbled level, turned to the steps;
the house itself solid Victorian,
built when the town grew linen-prosperous
along the loughside free of factory smoke,
compelled by purpose of my careful trade
to value and preserve what might be lost,
awarding names, suggesting destinations,
I came that chill, appointed winter morning.

I reached the steps. I pressed the bell and waited.
A woman opened knowing why I'd come,
no fresh-cheeked country servant, no housekeeper,
the lady of the house by her demeanour,
a small neat woman in her middle years.
Welcomed, led to and left in the drawing room
till she returned with what I'd called to see,
my glance and step moved round, establishing,
by furniture and what was on the walls,
the tidemarks of the rippled generations,
the well-scuffed armchairs tasselled, the low sofa,
the well-worn carpet and some later rugs,
the tables, the piano piled with sheet music,
the rows of Scott and Dickens in the bookcase,
a steel engraving of that man at shoeing,
a watercolour of our native mountains
in the safe manner of ninety years ago,
a few Arundel prints in Oxford frames,
two, gilded, oval, of tinted shawl and whiskers,
flanking the mirror over the mantelpiece,
the marble clock stacked round with photographs
of tight-lipped officers from several wars,
a hockey team with cup and folded arms.

I said, when she came back and set the box
on a side table, fingering its wrapping cloth,

that I should not appear too curious,
turning to the window which faced the sea,
'That's a fine view you have, across the bay.'
'But from that other window,' she replied,
indicating with ring-fingered hand,
'you see the hill. That is the view we like.'
I turned and checked, rose garden, trellised wall,
rising abruptly to a timbered prospect,
bare cliff behind it, against the heavy sky.
'It must have been,' I said, 'say, last October,
a splendid sight with all those autumn tints.'
'But we prefer the look of it in spring.' –
I took that as some family opinion
taken by a vote some Halloween –
'I hope the people after us will take care
of the plantation, and not let it go
to be a public park for children to ruin,
breaking the branches, pulling all the bluebells.'
Was then the place for sale? Already sold?
That's why she'd rung the office. Who were we
who liked the view: her husband, mother, sister?
The questions tangled. She'd unwrapped the box
and opened it. Examining the object,
lifting and turning, with my pocket lens
and jargon of technique, I followed through
the ritual of occasion to my sentence,
padding it out with ready parallels.
She listened, nodded, took it from my hand
laid it in and closed the box again.

Our business ended, stepping to the door,
when she had offered coffee or a sherry
which I'd declined with press of other calls,
I spared a comment for the watercolour.
She told me nothing of its provenance;
it had no history; it was always there.

Along the passage my glance lingered on
a crayon portrait by a hand I knew,

familiar in these parts. The artist seldom
dated his work. His style had never altered.
I could not tell just when this had been drawn.
'He caught the likeness but completely missed
the personality. That young man there' —
She had me puzzled; nephew, cousin, kinsman?
Not closer clearly with that adjective —
'is not, as he has drawn him, slightly built.
He is strong and broad; there is no doubt of that.' —
My quick thoughts flickered; I could not relate
this dateless drawing to a time in her life,
or work out what relation she bore to it —
'This never would suggest the Armstrong shoulders.' —
The notion shook me. Had he been a forward?
Or was such bulk the family male tradition?
Young in the drawing, what was his age now?

Checking my confusion, I followed her,
 the unasked questions now dismissed forever.
The last stride brought us to the broad front door;
she opened, thanked me, pointed to the right.
'You should go that way down; it's more direct.'

A difficult man

He was boring often with his laborious talk
describing some technical process in tedious detail,
though admittedly well-briefed in his narrow reading;
annoying too in his stubborn postures, for instance,
not painting in watercolours because he was thinking in oils.
Even the meticulous manner in which he folded his scarf
before putting on his overcoat seemed surely designed
indefinitely to delay his overdue departure,
yet we liked him because he was honest and loyal.

One summer Sunday evening over forty years ago
when we had had a day's picnic at Donegore
he got as far as outlining the church on the canvas board,
while we had chattered, picked wildflowers, read the headstones.
We missed the last bus home and had to walk to Parkgate
to catch a later bus by another route back to town,
and as we followed steadily the long slope of the land,
past houses with slated roofs and whitewashed gables,
corrugated rusty sheds and older thatched outbuildings,
hedges and trees and fields of potatoes and grazing
were still in the sidelong light of the setting sun,
he pointed out and named the coloured shadows
on roof, on gable, on pillar, on every surface,
in the dark furrows between the growing rows,
among the cut swathes of hay and the seeding grasses,
the colour of sunlight enriched by the colour of shadows;
not tedious now the instances, the repetitions,
demonstrating the features of the Impressionist Theory.
Because of that day I look always for colour in shadow;
very few, before or after, have taught me so much.

Drypoint

A final-year student at the Art School
a gangling fellow loping in his stride,
his paintings skilful but derivative,
his experimental carvings clumsy,
only his drypoints – the copper plate in his pocket
to be drawn upon directly with the needle –
communicated a delicate personal vision,
those and one brief Imagist poem
about a hen and a farm cart.

It was because of this last
he suddenly took me for an enemy.
I'd had it printed without asking his leave
in an ephemeral sheet a friend published.
He stumped in one evening without a word,
– have you ever tried to speak
to one who remains obdurately silent? –
lurched round the shelves and walls gathering
his unframed canvasses and wooden figures,
and clumped down the stairs for the last time.
The drypoints he could not remove
because I had paid him a few shillings for them.

Within the year he was dead;
I did not even know that he was ill.
I did not hear of this for several months,
and now, with others dead who knew him,
I do not know if anyone else remembers him.

I had learnt that it was not
the printing of the poem
which had annoyed him
but where it had been printed,
a circumstance I could not comprehend,
for most young poets like to see their verses
in print anywhere.

Framed now a long time
his print of the ponderous sow
is among the few pictures in my possession
which I always keep somewhere at hand,
but the last line of the poem
is his best epitaph:
'the hen that laid away'.

The test

Sped by the British Council
to study museum techniques,
the gentle little Indian
with the large dark mournful eyes
(32, curator, married, 3 children,
from a museum in Bengal)
paced the public galleries,
inspecting the picturestore, the printroom,
the workroom, the back stairs, the lift,
and returned to my office
where I waited for his questions.

One problem he raised with some seriousness,
'You have Indian workers employed here.
Were there no Englishmans waiting?'
I replied that after interviews
the best applicants were appointed,
those most suitable for our purpose,
carefully conscious that I made
no reference to race or colour.

He nodded a tepid approval,
his large dark eyes still mournful,
showing less enthusiasm
than I had expected.
'Did you not give them a taste?'
A split-second permitted me
to grasp that he pronounced the word test
with a diphthong.

Then he continued with deliberation,
'In these things there is often backdoorism.
A man may have a letter from the Minister.
If you make him a test
this is an advantage.'

Being Irish, from a tribal society myself,
I appreciated the difficulty, recalling
the scrum of backdoorists I had known
at home, both cunning and clumsy,
and thought that if this brown little man
had come to learn modern techniques
he certainly knew the old ones.

Calling on Peadar O'Donnell at Dungloe

I remember striding through the August twilight
along a narrow lane from house to house;
a crowd of lads were hurling loud and shouting,
and once a black calf gave a mournful cry.

It seemed the long track round that we had taken
over a rough ground higher than the bog.
Three fields away foam topped the distant breakers.
Storm's opposition flogged us both dog-tired.

Then darkness dropped, and window after window
offered no trace of colour. We went on,
slow pacing now, and painfully admonished
by plaintive gulls above the ocean's din.

We reached the three small houses and the gate
which faced the place the drive swung to the right.
Now far too late to make our call we argued.
There was no blink of light in any room.

But halfway up the drive we glimpsed the writer
still working in the garden with his wife;
I shouted and he straightened up to answer,
and in the gloom his fine head glimmered white.

The ballad

When I sought out the Cottage Hospital
basking in sun beside the village stream,
the matron absent, a smiling sister
led me upstairs to my aged woman
sitting by her bed,
her two companions prone;
one slept, the other stirred and smiled.

My aged woman peered, puckering her lids.
Loudly I named myself and when we met last.
She recognised but asked
had I been bearded then.
Sure of her ground now, slipped to Robbie Burns,
great-hearted poet, and one piece he wrote
about his latter end, addressing his Maker,
better than all.

Then with a smile, 'I put you
in the same room with him and those I like.
My memory's all in tatters. Here and there
I have my cameos. You wrote a poem
about the sunrise over the bay.'
That was nearly forty years ago,
part of a long poem on the place.
I knew her slightly then, a small woman,
behind the counter of her shop;
recalled the nature of our talk;
with frequent visits after
becoming my Sybil of the Glens.

Proud but embarrassed,
I turned the talk to something else,
a topic I had tried with elderly folk
where a response was possible,
and phrased the title of that ballad
current in her youth among her kind;

I have called up frequent echoes
in places I'd thought likely,
those now over pension age
who share memories of our national past.

She knew it as I had expected;
the opening lines came easily, then limped;
then confidence found wings,
brisk verses followed, faltered. . .
a prose account filled in the missing lines.
Hands before her face,
she blamed her tattered memory;
'You can't put your own words for the poet's words,
for his words are the poem.'

Then snatching at a run the final stanzas,
lifted her white face and smiled,
took my hand, thanked me for calling,
for having made her day.
Humbly, moved, I left,
now more than her day made.

The clink of rhyme

A student here, from Ballintoy,
a laughing fair-haired country boy,
felt now and then fit to employ
      his Sunday leisure
in turning verses to enjoy
      poetic pleasure.

I showed him how with little cost
his thought was better far engrossed
in the blank verse of Robert Frost,
      and as a duck
takes to the burn in which it's tossed
      he tried his luck.

The lines came supple, steady, clear,
true to the country atmosphere.
There was no flowery discourse here
      but honest phrasing;
and half a dozen times that year
      he sought my praising.

But once he read his verse o'er
to some oul' *caillaigh* at her door
who had a name in three or four
      townlands for rhyming,
that he might hear how much he'd score
      by her skilled timing.

Awhile she listened to him dumb,
with not so much as Haw or Hum;
then, sucking at her toothless gum,
      she said, 'I think
I'd rather hae the thochts that come
      in lines that clink.'

Folk custom

Our foolish neighbour farther up the hill,
already twice before the Bench, again
has earned more trouble with his private still;
he wore a *pad* to like a well-trod lane,
running his neck into law's ready noose,
who only made *poteen* for table use.

It had been something if he'd flashed the stuff
at every *céilí* round the countryside
and from the eager orders cleared enough
to pay his debts or gain a second bride,
but he'd no better wit nor more to do
than stretch on Sundays *full*, along the *brú*.

It's not his misdemeanour that affronts;
we all have careless follies to confess;
be up before the Petty Sessions once,
and not a man will rate a *haet* the less:
it's that we know of smarter men that wrought
at stilling all their days were never caught.

MacDonnell's question

Raging on Duneneeny while the smoke
spired from the thatches round the boat-thronged bay –
across the treacherous sound of Corrie Vrecken,
where Brechan's fifty curraghs were all swamped –
the bay of Rathlin, Raghery of the Oaks,
he stormed along the cliff-turf impotent,
while children, women, cattle, stores of grain
flared to the zenith by the English torch
and cannonry of Norris, Essex' man –
the cruel Drake was of that company;
the great Queen heard of it at Kenilworth –
this Sorley Boy, this Charley Yellowhair,
of Clan MacDonnell chief, Lord of the Route,
sixth son of Alexander of Cantyre,
vast troubler of that great Queen's deputies –
he could not write his name, but touched the quill
his secretary penned despatches with.

And where Sir Arthur Chichester kneels down,
facing his kneeling lady in that high tomb
in Carrickfergus, old St Nicholas' Church,
over the smaller effigy of Sir John
praying his pardon, MacDonnell stopped to gape –
James, son of Sorley, knighted by James the Sixth
a brave, courageous, hospitable fellow –
'Whar gat ye your heid, Sir John? I mind the day
I clippt it aff ye, when you'd hae ambushed me.'
Those footnote addicts, the historians,
assert this is some legendary fiction,
offering proper dates as positive proof,
and anyhow James never spoke in Scots
but in the Gaelic of the Western Isles.
I do not care. My heart takes it as true;
there's little justice enough in our history.

The house on the hill

This house built tall, half burnt and raised again
here on the round crest of an Antrim brae,
has earthed the dreams and schemes of many men
and watched far more than seasons pass this way.

For us then first the chief who turned his coat
when the old faith endured a cruel shock,
and in the dripping wood not too remote
a hunted priest served mass upon a rock;
and with the loyal lining now displayed
new words were found to chip into the stone
that covers where the Papist bones were laid,
the details, dates and heraldry his own.

So the rough Gaels became fine gentlemen,
the place marked clearly on the coaching chart;
the gothic lodge, the drive, the high-walled garden,
the pillared gates bespoke this change of heart.
Then, by degrees of breeding's planned ascent,
the new age beckons, old clan shadows lift;
the flushed, wigged master drives to parliament,
or sets his wit against the wit of Swift.

The elder son succeeds, secure in state
pores over those long letters from Bengal,
stands bravely up to Grattan in debate
or prunes his roses on the trellised wall.
His two well-dowried daughters married soon,
into wide paddocks, artificial lakes.
This is Augustan peace. It is high noon.
The wager's now for ever-rising stakes.

Along the steep lane where the gate lodge broods
beneath the thorn, beside the shattered gate,
where only a lost traveller intrudes
or some snare-setting local working late,

there is a cottage just above the spring,
where a man standing by his workshop door
will, if you wait, remember everything
that happened to the big house long before.

He can recall when he was just a child
what older people told him of the place;
Castle, they called it, with great coaches styled
where trailing dresses swept with haughty grace.
He shuffles back among his eighty years
to times the house changed hands, from whom to whom;
the timber merchants' French carved screen, he hears,
is still the wonder of the drawing room,
left with much else after he sold it to
an admiral who bore a famous name –
it was a kinsman with another crew
whose rebel-death gave all that family's fame.

The wheel spins faster now. They come and go;
the Glasgow publican whose lucky bet
brought horses, grooms, till with a sudden blow
the money-lenders seized all for his debt.
It seems the house lay under some old curse,
for once fire gutted upper rooms inside,
just when the painters and the plasterers
had made all trim and tidy for a bride.

The man who bought it planned to renovate it,
planted new trees or had some cut away,
proved it too big, remotely situated,
its heavy upkeep more than he could pay.
The next, on city architect's report,
raised a blind wall to balance the left wing,
with castellated turrets, tennis court,
but never stayed to see a second spring.

There was a spell when what was once a home
became a lit hotel with board and sign,
and tweedy-golfers, fishermen, would come

in motors roaring up the lane to dine;
and the rooms tangled ancient memories
with gramophones and jazz, all out of key
with gracious gestures and grave courtesies,
laced with gay Dublin Castle repartee.

The Church then purchased it. The lily pond
with squat Greek gods like opera-set or play,
the gravelled courtyard where the four-in-hand
brought word of Bunkershill or Castlereagh,
is seldom vexed by any other stir
than that of nuns whose dignity and grace,
whose hooded forms, lend quiet character
to what was once a change-tormented place.

Although the fabulous slab may still be found
amid the old graveyard's tussocked grass and stone
in that high house, a landmark miles around,
the Gael's faith slippers back to claim its own.

This Antrim air in summer

This country's air is cleansing to the heart;
Atlantic-fresh, and washed with spray and rain,
it leaps off leaves and blusters down the lane;
in frolic gusto sometimes spins apart
to pluck at peat-reek, bearing in its stride
that friendly tang across a sheltered glen;
whips flax-dam's ripples to a thrusting tide,
or heads the drifting swansdown back again;
shaped by the running lines of crag and hill,
combs tossed bog-cotton tufts, lifts flagging crow,
stripping cloud's corner, clears the bare blue sky,
or, drunk on hawthorn, hoards the heat until,
startled at sudden thunder stumping by,
it cuffs the thistle with a rocking blow.

Autumn gale

All day a strong gale rushed north west by north,
herding stripped leaves in corners, wiping dry
the bare wet lanes, and over crumbled earth
spreading a crisper surface, scudding by
and flicking skirts of shadow on the ground,
till breath was an adventure bravely borne,
despite the bitter winter's forecast found
in crowded berries on the whistling thorn.

Then as the sun dropped down, his tilted light
raking the rocking treetops, the black crows
whirling in gusts, were each that moment bright
against the wind's face as they sank or rose,
as this which seemed some March-fresh interval
played havoc with the season's dying fall.

The old mill-race

From the high stream the water poured and forced
an unstaunched torrent through the gaping boards
which fenced in better times the streams apart;
but now it struck the lower constant river
with such a jet there shot a fountain-head,
a crest of spray, which carried to the light
a bush of blossom white like a summer tree
wearing its golden tinctures of the sun
a trembling moment on its quivering twigs;
as suddenly becoming, these withdrawn,
a snowy bush that shivered with chill flakes.
O bush of hawthorn blossom, bush of snow,
holding frail shape of evershifting atoms,
must I spin also, lost, into the sea?

The descent

We slipped and slithered down the thick-timbered hill,
snatched branch which snapped like tinder, broke away,
struck heel on leaf imprinted flat on clay
which sledded us precipitate, until
fist fumbled tussock on a crumbling sill
and we dropped depths we'd not have dared in play,
groping, with twig-whipped face, through chequered day,
dislodging stones which bounded, rolled, fell still.

With aching ankles, sinews wrenched in fright,
stained fingers, palms streaked by grey, yielding moss,
we thrust through the last thicket and stood free
and, safe on sod secure, remarked the height
we'd lurched down, cancelled out, amazed to see
high pool of sky a heron soars across.

The souterrain

We cut the sod. We dug the heavy mould
to bare the stones which stronger folk have laid
over their tunnelled dwelling. Pick and spade
reminded shoulder, forearm, we grew old,
save for the lad whose easy gestures told
that this was something near his daily trade.
Absolved by age, the nodding farmer made
a ready bet we'd crack no crock of gold.

When the large stone was scraped, was bared to light
and shifted as the soil began to spill
in sandglass trickle slowly out of sight,
as the dark passage beckoned, deep and still,
for a hushed spell no crock of gold could buy
we brinked the silent pit of mystery.

Palimpsest

I pace these lanes where progress and decay
scribble wry palimpsest across the scene;
the raw byre gable shoulders concrete-clean
where once a reeking midden seeped away;
the tractor treads have sliced into the clay
but left a middle track still clover green;
once homesteads, now those *wallsteads* bulge and lean,
and nettles flower where children used to play.

And all those old men gone, these slow old men,
whose thumbs were thick with skills I could not share,
at loanen-end or gate, shall not again
forgather, nor at church door or the fair,
the shepherd, scythesman, blacksmith, carpenter,
as life drains surely down the tree-dark glen.

The Christmas Rhymers, Ballynure 1941: an old woman remembers

The Christmas Rhymers came again last year,
wee boys with blackened faces at the door,
not like those strapping lads that would appear,
dressed for the mummers' parts in times before,
to act the old play on the kitchen floor;
at warwork now or fighting overseas,
my neighbours' sons; there's hardly one of these
that will be coming back here any more.

I gave them coppers, bid them turn and go;
and as I watched that rueful regiment
head for the road, I felt that with them went
those songs we sang, the rhymes we used to know,
heartsore imagining the years without
The Doctor, Darkie, and Wee Divil Doubt.

Encounter with R.J. Welch, the antiquary

On tram's topdeck – in Nineteen Twenty-Three –
as I sat reading in my usual way –
the passing townscape known familiarly,
there was no need to let attention stray –
a bearded man who sat beside me peered
at what I read. I smirked in some unease,
a Sitwell book, *Bucolic Comedies*.
His curiosity seemed undeterred.

'What are you reading?' Coolest of replies,
I showed him all the title page declares.
'Bucolic has to do with country things.
Reading in trams will ruin your young eyes.'
And with that warning suddenly he springs
out of his seat and rushes down the stairs.

The house at Ballyholme

I

This was my grannie's house, far different
from ours at home, much farther from the road,
with wide bay windows spaciously endowed,
a long path to the door, which bravely bent
right round the house, with gardens front and rear,
that at the front in summer sure to please
with scent and colour lavish everywhere,
that round the back half grass, half apple trees.

Yet from that richness my prime picture comes
with lion's cage, with caravan and clown,
with prancing horses, loud bassoons and drums,
as down those jolting pebbles to the gate
my father's shoulder bore my infant weight
when Duffy's Circus flourished into town.

II

I knew that place but never felt it mine,
paid frequent visits, often holidayed,
and lived there half a year when I was nine;
on those front steps my mitching was betrayed.
In spring I think of that laburnum tree
whose pods were poison; it was sinister;
that small back garden orchard was for me
a magic island, I was Crusoe there.

Within the walls my wits hold little more
than private cupboards where my grannie'd hide
and fumble over secrets hers alone,
red kitchen tiles, scrubbed table, the back door
at which that black dog Jim would twitch and moan,
mourning his master when our uncle died.

My widowed mother

Ten years a widow, my old mother's mind
became fragmented; first the box played tricks
with horses in the hall; then she would find
comedians' features quickly intermix
with those of ancient friends, and once she thought
I was her husband, callous and inhuman
when quite regardless of her rights I'd brought
under her roof a young and comely woman.

We drove her to the Mental Hospital,
passing a new-built chapel on the way,
which noting, she considered 'well-behaved';
a shrewd remark, scant evidence at all
her envied choice of words had gone astray
which since my childhood held my wits enslaved.

Bandstand

Remark the empty bandstand in the park,
bird-droppings on the iron balustrade
and dead leaves in the corners. After dark
when the bell rings and rangers lock the gate
the lilting games the laughing children played
are little sleepy ghosts, and hardly wait
till the last footfall dies before they find
a quiet twig to hammock their repose,
and the quick birds are nested with their kind;
but sometimes when the wind gusts up and blows
dark clouds across and off the rocking moon,
between the gusts, in lulls within the storm,
you'll hear by chance a low drum-major tune
from shadowy men in moon-pale uniform.

For Roberta in the garden

I know when you are at your happiest,
kneeling on mould, a trowel in your glove;
you raise your eyes and for a moment rest;
you turn a young-girl's face, like one in love.

Intent, entranced, this hour, in gardening,
surely to life's bright process you belong.
I wonder, when you pause, you do not sing,
for such a moment surely has its song.

The hedgehog: for R.

With shrewd snout the hedgehog
snuffles across the lawn
over the long shadows
of stilted hollyhock;
unpredicted presence
its purposes unguessed,
threading a tiny life,
heart pulsing, hungry, warm,
slack spines dragging against
the prospering clover,
unresting, out of reach.

Its secret triggers set,
it seemed a symbol
for all timid strangeness,
all shy wildness, alert
to defend itself by
privacy, withdrawal;
a fellow creature lurked
within your heart and mine.

At the newsagent's

I

At about 8.15 a.m.
a police reservist called
at the newsagent's
for his morning paper.

When he came out
he met a spray of bullets
which killed him and wounded
his companion waiting in the car.

One of the bullets cut a hole
in the upper panel
of the glass and metal door
which had closed behind him.

I go to this newsagent's
several times a week
to pick up my magazines
and buy pipe tobacco.

And every time
I push open that door,
though the shattered glass
has since been replaced,

I think fleetingly
of the bullet hole;
this, I suppose, might be considered
'an objective correlative'.

II

Colleagues of the murderer
or murderers – I do not know
how many guns were then fired –
captured, sentenced, imprisoned, insisted
that they were 'political prisoners';
and to assert the status they claimed
neither washed, shaved, nor cut their hair;
they wore no clothes except a blanket,
and smeared their cell-walls with their shit.
This exercise was known as 'On the Blanket'
or 'The Dirty Protest'.

Some months later
ten of the younger prisoners
starved themselves to death
to sustain the protest.

None of these happenings,
widely communicated through
the popular media,
even flickers, however faintly,
among the reflecting grimaces
in that glass door.

The bombed public house

This was the pub where I once took that playwright
famous for broadcast brawl but witty sober.
He warned me going in he had no money,
and took a single pint of several offered.

This was the pub where I was called to meet
the foreign poet; when he asked my age
he kissed me on both cheeks and called me father.

This was the pub where the small bald barman
always called me Doctor or Professor
on my infrequent visits, being neither.

When this interior is restored, recovered
with fashionable surfaces and textures
will any mirror echo such reflections
or cushioned corner's covers bounce them back?

Executives third tier

The morning after the seminar
I met a colleague whose glance I had caught
in that maze of programme budgetting,
input analysis and cost-effectiveness.

So, knowing my man, I stopped to enquire
How are your parameters this morning?
Nearly frozen off. And your infrastructure?
I haven't quantified it yet.

And the two elderly Luddites
strode off to their separate departments,
smiling serenely, each caressing
the spanner in his pocket.

Administration

He is a knowing fellow who devotes
his busy pen to brisk peremptory notes,
Your Observations re; Consult; Discuss.
You should not think such scripts ridiculous;
our age's judgement is, he who creates
most memoranda, best administrates.
So paste these on the broad blind, slat by slat;
the battle orders of the bureaucrat.

By air to Birmingham on a mid June evening

Lough Beg a sungleam, little Coney Island,
the Irish hedges powdered still
with blossom on blackthorn.

We have shot up
too quickly for my wits to draw
the comforting webs of association;
for the moment I take what my eyes offer.

The Unseen God,
who so has hoisted us out of time
and disengaged us from reality,
has already promised us
Speed, Altitude, Arrival back in time,
and foretold the weather of our coming.

Out of the mist over the city valley –
because of that mist pervasive
and the paths our past took,
I have never once been able to comprehend
my city from above and fix an image for it;
walking through, it breaks into fragments of existence,
mine and others I have knowledge of –
we cut through to a glacial landscape,
passing in sunlight over a near-white floor,
not brilliant white, not painter's gesso panel,
but rather grey of fleece, of sunwarm fleece,
a furrowed field of snow, its contours padded
with furrows of rounded clods
by some gigantic ploughshare tossed,
a stiff ocean of thumb-puttied waves –
I once had a ship model in a glass box
with painted putty waves, their crests
in series flecked with white for foam.

Here free by now
from flight's involvement, subjugation to
abrupt event, engined beyond me,
riding easy, the mind unbelts, unclenches,
and moves over experience
smoothly, slotting-in sensation.

Our angle changes, the landscape tilts
as sometimes land spills off the board;
and its edges seem
like teasled wool, like tufts on barbs.
Then as the cloud spins thin
and drifts away in wisps, we glimpse
the sea below, the actual ocean,
wrinkled – Tennyson's word. I observe
only what I have words for – with tiny puckers plucked,
which indicate
small vessels urgent tugged from port to port.

A wavering line of sand fringes green and pewter –
when I see a shoreline I always think
of invaders running keels in,
leaping breast high, thigh deep,
Greeks, Vikings, Romans mostly;
a farm cart in Sicily showed
Caesar's legions in that act;
invading Britain the coarse letters said.
Like others from the east, like all others;
but my folk landed dryshod.

Cloud draws its cover over.
Above, a level sky like any sky
over a plain. There are two skies,
earth's sky and ours:
the red horizon smudged, frayed,
against the west.

Down through mist.
Above, a band of gold
receding:
a map of roads below
of a strange solid country.

Out of the daylight now
lamps sparkle like stars
in an inverted firmament –
I've waited years to use that word –
the constellations too regular to be true.

Propellers rainbow:
the dark blades emerge
through flickering shutters.
Street lights and dotted scribbles.
Close-meshed suburbs glow.
Long spangled roads belt over the dark land,
with here and there a blob of bloody light;
and tiny insects
with smears of light ahead, astern,
pulse and pause along dim arteries.

Our moth is gathered into
the airport's web and tent of light.
We replace the magazine
in its elastic net. . .
The engine alters.
Lettered lights instruct.

We are on the point
of returning
to ourselves.

Rotterdam

Out of the grey wet sand
the bright concourse of tall buildings,
neon-garlanded, with flood-lit fountains,
thrusts away the vast anonymous sky.

The well-dressed shop windows
are full of expensive consumer goods.
A bastion of metal cargo-containers
has been erected along the dockside.

And in the small moat outside
the Boymans-Van Beuningen Museum
a gentle breeze wafts a blue plastic bucket
and a large red ball into a corner.

To the People of Dresden

Your famous city stood, plucked out of time,
a dream-pavilion set in porcelain,
where the masked dancers paced in stately mime
with grace no later age can now attain.
Then towards disaster all seemed swiftly drawn,
your cruel fire-storm fuelling men's fears,
to shards all shattered, all those dancers gone,
in the dark Europe of my middle years.

But now that darkness breaks, and I have stood,
shouldered with thousands in your Altmarkt Square,
to swear my silent oath of brotherhood,
and join my lonely prayer to your vast prayer
that by the common will of common men
no war shall ever darken day again.

Winter park

All growth securely grappled to the ground,
by frost-crisp paths I make my usual round;
and at the circular bed where roses stood
that now are stubbed to spiky stumps of wood
a young man raking takes the time to toss
some praise for hardy weather as I pass;
I call assent but slow no step to tell
that my own husbandry is going well.

On the preservation of work sheets

It should not matter how I shaped my lines,
hit on a cadence; shuffled adjectives,
replaced a showy word with one that gives
a truer texture, or, precise, defines
a signal smudged by clumsy countersigns,
or altered phrase to mark a change of gear
when word proposing word at once combines
to make some level of intention clear.

Should I expose each stutter of my thought,
each accident of memory or of sense,
through which the structure to completion brought
is seen as weapon forged in self defence?
No more absurd than that I'd hoard and store
the fringe of filings on the workshop floor.

Dissertation I

Tomorrow with his notes a man will come
enquiring when I wrote that verse or this,
where such and such an image sprouted from,
if I concur with his analysis,
the day, the hour, what infantile event,
and in what order should these carry weight;
so, explicating what I must have meant,
I'll flick my notebooks through to check the date.

I'll give what help I can. But humbly, pleased
that anyone should show the least concern
for words I named that secret springs released
out of the shadowy culverts of my mind,
eager for what I've sought so long to learn,
and anxious too for what we both may find.

Dissertation II

At least, with the dentist,
I am aware of the drill
spinning endlessly,
though the preliminary needle
cut the threads
of consequential pain.

But with the research student
in the next room, reading
the letters, the manuscripts,
I certainly feel no bone-tremor;
yet anxiety travels
along nerves not used to traffic.

I can rinse and spit out
the scorched gritty particles
but though my bone-structure is strong,
I bleed too easily.

In recollection of Drumcliffe, September 1948

The years spin quicker since that day I stood
to watch the poet's coffin take to earth
a second time, in kinship's neighbourhood
which gave his proud imagination birth;
and my clenched homage knelt to cross and tower,
to those dark famous hills which, till time ends,
must wear the shapes conferred by vatic power,
the power that fleshed our legends and his friends.

Although I could not share his thoughts, and choose
instead a faith in man's progressive range,
finding his stance and temper alien,
I carry thence what I shall never lose,
his chanted cadence, and the right to change
the masks with which I face my fellowmen.

First honey

My mind drifts back to those far days that bred
the heart-light lyric leaping off the thought
some flicking twig or wing provoked unsought
and easily nested in a rhyme-rife head.
Now strangely, from youth's hopes and hazards free,
the verses come much slower, with a tone
closer to speech than song, their quality
of time's four seasons, this grave last alone.

Pulse-proven, wiser, maybe, but the mood
once lyric bright is now diffused and grey,
each blurred sun rises on a briefer day;
not green braird thrusting but rain darkened corn;
so I look back with ready gratitude
to that first honey won from blossomed thorn.

Retreaded rhymes

Henceforth my slow wits I must only spend
to phrase affection or to mourn a friend;
to state the convolutions of my thought
in quiet verse deliberately wrought,
leaving the coloured crags' romantic line
for humbler acre fairly mapped as mine;
stranger to passion, never strongly moved
by those emotions use has not approved;
responsive to the year's flow, spring to fall,
saluting winter at the end of all. . .

So ran my programme forty years ago,
in safe iambics, *sotto voce*, slow;
and since the butts are close, the circles wide,
I've kept on target, and am satisfied
when I recall behind the placid verse
a man still stands whose attitude declares
his loyalty to hope, unquenched belief,
despite the incidence of age or grief,
in men's rare-hinted possibility
of being just, compassionate and free.

I struck these verses also in a set
of plodding lines which offer comfort yet;
though pill-propelled, unsteady in my gait,
and conscious daily of my mortal state,
they sing their sense forever in my head:
O windblown grass upon the mounded dead,
O seed in crevice of the frost-split rock,
the power that fixed your root shall take us back
though endlessly through aeons we are thrust
as luminous or unreflecting dust.

Lines for a dead alderman

Justice is done in the end,
the rascal who had his day
to party and prejudice friend,
lodged in non-partisan clay.
As the mourners drive away
they leave that bundle of lies
to the earthworms' enterprise.

But, Lord, it is long to wait
till the wrong that that man did
and the hurt born of his hate
lies under the coffin-lid;
the earth may never be rid
of that wrong this side of time
if I let it tarnish my rhyme.

St Stephen's Day

St Stephen's Day, the air is warm,
fair, early prelude to the spring,
though finches pick at withered haws
and stiff-necked swans beat leaden wing.

The old men bundled in their coats
creep out to greet the peeping sun,
as if, like jewel-headed toads,
they'd splintered winter's flinty stone.

Notes

'The portrait', p.5: 'a crayon portrait by a hand I knew' – William Conor RHA (1881–1968).

'The ballad', p.13: 'The man from God knows where', from *The Coming of the Earls* (1918) by Florence L. Wilson.

'The clink of rhyme', p.15: *caillaigh,* an old woman.

'Folk custom', p.16: *pad,* path; *poteen,* illicit liquor; *céilí,* social call for conversation and music; *full,* drunk; *brú,* bank at side of lane or field; *haet,* a whit.

'MacDonnell's question', p.17: Sorley Boy (1505–1590), Chief of Clandonnell.

The massacre on Rathlin took place in 1575.

Sir Arthur Chichester (1563–1625), Governor of Carrickfergus, Admiral of Lough Neagh, one of the leading organisers and the chief beneficiary of the Plantation of Ulster. His funerary monument was commissioned and probably delivered during his lifetime. His elder brother Sir John was killed in a skirmish at Altfrackin, near Carrickfergus, in 1597; Sir James MacDonnell was poisoned in 1601.

'The house on the hill', p.18: 'mass upon a rock', 'the Altar in the Woods', Glendun.

'Kinsman with another crew', Sir Roger Casement.

'The souterrain', p.25: underground stone-built passage and chamber, near Doagh, in the valley of the Sixmilewater, where many of these have been found.

'Palimpsest', p.26: *wallstead,* roofless ruin of house or cottage.

'Tree-dark glen', the upper reaches of the Glens now undergoing afforestation.

'The Christmas Rhymers', p.27: substance of this from an old Ballyeaston woman in 1941.

'The Doctor, Darkie and Wee Divil Doubt', characters from mummers' play performed in S.E. Antrim.

'Encounter with R.J. Welch', p.28: Robert Welch (1859–1936) geologist, photographer.

'To the People of Dresden', p.43: I took part in a peace demonstration in February 1959 on the anniversary of Allied air raids, 13–14 February 1945.

'Retreaded rhymes', p.50: The first ten lines are from 'Interim' (*No Rebel Word,* 1948); the last five lines from 'Freehold' in *Lagan* 1946.